y, Budapest is a city of two million inhabitants situated e middle of Europe, in that it is roughly halfway between Atlantic Ocean and the Ural Mountains. For 2000 years have been settlements in the area presently occupied by pest, but only in 1873 were these united as the Hung- capital. At that time the country was three times the it is now, although, as the eastern half of the Austro- garian Monarchy, it was not fully independent. The Car- an Basin is divided by the River Danube into a hilly and lating western part and a mainly flat eastern one.

The southeastern corner of the Carpathian Basin marked the furthest point of penetration achieved by Western culture, Gothic architecture and the Reformation. Further east was the world of Byzantium, the western limit of which is Budapest. The Danube also divides Hungary culturally, including Buda and Pest: the character of Pest people differs from that of Buda residents. Visitors to the city sometimes feel that they are travelling in time when they walk the streets and squares of Buda and Pest. This illustrated guide will perhaps help visitors remember the things they have seen.

2

3

The city consists of two parts: Buda in the hills and Pes
the plain. Pest is 1000 years old, while the Buda Castle D
rict became a town seven and a half centuries ago. The
mer Royal Palace towers above the town (**2**). Building w
began on it around the year 1300 and was finished abc
century ago. In January 1945 it was almost completely
stroyed – revealing remains of the Medieval castle ben
the Baroque palace. It served as the court of kings belon
to the Anjou, Luxembourg and Habsburg dynasties. F
1458 until 1485 it was occupied by the elected king Mat
Corvinus, and from 1920 until 1944 by the elected re
Miklós Horthy. Today the building houses museums, a lib
and a theatre. Today this former seat of elevated persor
is occupied by tourists taking photographs from the ec
trian statue of *Prince Eugene of Savoy* (**4**), and from
Funicular Railway with its gentle pace (**3**).

5

ı has been justly admired. At the time of King Matthias
n humanists declared that Florence was the finest city on
plains, Venice the finest city by the sea, and Buda the
t city in the hills.
ome extent they could regard Buda as their own, since
hias's wife was the Neapolitan Beatrix of Aragon, and the
himself was a patron of Italian culture, worthy of a place
side the Medicis. Leonardo himself was among those re-
ng his patronage. Under King Matthias Buda became an
rtant outpost of Renaissance learning.

The palace's two large courtyards are connected by a gateway guarded by stone lions, near which a fountain by Alajos Stróbl immortalizes *King Matthias Out Hunting* (**5**). A few decades ago this interesting group of sculptures – with its hints of Romanticism, Impressionism and Art Nouveau, as well as its different materials – seemed hopelessly outdated. But visitors who have grown up on Pop Art, Hyper-realism and Postmodernism are now prone to favour this literary-type turn-of-the-century work on the walls of the Hungarian National Gallery courtyard.

6

8

Medieval Buda consisted of four
five longish streets – these make up
Castle District. Formerly, Germans, H
garians, Italians, and Jews lived here,
later on Turks as well. There were
large churches, which were turned i
mosques after the Turks captured
town in 1541, and two synagogues,
smaller of which is now a museum.

The Turks did not lay siege to Buda,
walked in as possible allies. In the
Buda did not become a "suburb of
kish Vienna", but instead a run-d
border fortress of the far-flung Otto
empire. It was at this time that the d
of the fine Medieval town and palace
gan. Most of the Castle District
destroyed when Christian armies re
tured it from the Turks in 1686.
Much remains, however: 18th-cen
reconstructions of 15th-century d
ing-houses, with old details. These
mainly to be found in Úri utca, Or
ház utca and Fortuna utca (**6-8**).
bronze equestrian statue shows G
ral András Hadik (**10**), Maria Ther
commander who captured Berlin.

9

similar town centres remain in Eu-
e which have preserved their Medi-
features to such an extent, without
oming museums, bogus scenic idylls,
sometimes, gaudy tourist spectcles.
every fine old town, the Castle Dis-
reveals its charms. Those who live
e still lead quiet lives. They do not
ily move out, even if their homes are
fashioned.
ve in the Castle District means a
tige which is difficult to express in
etary terms.
resident, for example, was Baron
. Hatvany, an industrialist who had
ied classical philology. A patron
e arts, he lived in a *Classicist-style*
e next to the Neo-Romanesque
'ing of the Hungarian National
ives (**9**). In the 1930s the Hatvany
e served as the meeting-place for
s such as Thomas Mann and Béla
k. From the facade great figures
Antiquity – Seneca, Socrates, Livy,
Virgil – glanced down on these two
whose consciences obliged them
ive their respective countries in the
ist period.

10

11

12

It was here that Matthias Hunyadi m ried Beatrix of Aragon, the daughter the king of Naples, on December 2 1476. The feasting lasted until Twel Night, and was accompanied by jousti and other entertainments.

Some idea of what the *Matthias Chu* was like at this time is afforded by *South Door*, the so-called Mary Do (**12**). First mention of a Romanesc church on the site was in 1247, but building may have been older. Hav been rebuilt, enlarged and supplied w Gothic buttresses after 1350, it beca the church of the German burghers Buda. (The Hungarians lived in northern half of the town; theirs was former Church of St Mary Magdale of which only the tower now remains At the time of the large-scale constr tion work during the reigns of K Louis the Great (1342–82) and Si mund of Luxembourg (1387–143 the church, which was dedicated to Lady, was enlarged further, with the t er being added by King Matthias 1470. The stone embellishments on church are not Medieval, since tro struck the Matthias Church one h dred years later.

First it became the Suleiman mos then, after the recapture of the t from the Turks (in 1686), it became church of a Jesuit school. In addit fire, lightning, reconstruction in Baroque style, and the dissolution o Jesuit order in Hungary all had thei fects.

When, in 1867, the Hungarian na and the Austrian ruling house "c promised" with each other, recogn that neither could overcome the o Francis Joseph was crowned in church with the Holy Crown of Hun From this time onwards the building the Coronation Church – it was as such on just one later occasio 1916. The Gothic building (**11**) wa constructed and augmented by Fr Schulek in work which continue almost a quarter of a century, original details were brought to ligh incorporated in the overall effect. B lan Székely's painting of the in (**13**) was also in comformity with dieval survivals. The Matthias Chu Neo-Gothic,but is not new. Cons tion ended at the beginning of the century.

14

15

According to town legend, this sec of the Medieval town wall was defen by the fishermen's guild, although reality was probably different.

Gun emplacements were built her the 18th century, but no enemy peared: Austrian rule remained unc lenged. Between 1895 and 1902, gyes Schulek, who refashioned Matthias Church, designed this Ro esque-style fairy-tale castle on C Hill high above the Danube.

It was here that Alajos Stróbl's fi worked *equestrian statue* (**16**) of *Stephen the Saint* was erected, be the church.

On the summer days there is a bus life around the statue: vendors, r cians and comedians entertain fo visitors. Hungarians appear mainly sunset, most of them teenagers. A s tific survey would probably show more first kisses are given on the and under the arches of the Fisherr Bastion (**15**) than at any other The view from the Fishermen's Bas especially when the city is illuminat night, is a real crowd-puller (**14**). The terrace of the Hilton Hotel is close by.

ı Castle had real military signifi-
e, and was a more serious structure
the delicately-carved stones of the
ermen's Bastion.

e 20th century the walls of the old
ieval castle began to be unearthed,
attempts were made to show more
e picture bequeathed by the maker
e first creditable view of the town,
th-century German woodcut artist.
he south, very good views are af-
ed by the large circular bastion (the
della) and by the *Mace Tower* (**17**),
alled because of its shape.

by used to be the Tabán district, a
resque part of the town knocked
n earlier this century because it was
, unsanitary and associated with the
rworld. This was the Soho, China-
and Plaka of the old Budapest.
y the successors of the numerous
eating-houses here are less noto-
s, but just as good gastronomically.
flavours of real Hungarian cuisine
more accesssible in these restaur-
than in the expensive hotels.

16

17

18

There was once a high-born youn Venetian called Gerardus. He wanted t travel to the Holy Land to convert th heathens at the beginning of the secon millennium, but a vision directed hi northwards. He came to Hungary, wher he was warmly received by King Stephe who entrusted the education of his so Prince Imre, to him.

Gerardus, whom the Hungarians calle Gellért (**18**), brought the young man u to be a very devout Christian. When Ir re took a wife, he attached more impo tance to purity in marriage than did h successors. For this he was later cano ized, like his father, but when he died a hunting accident at an early age he l no heir. Gellért excelled in the fiel of authorship and Church organizatic and in the bloody and chaotic times t followed King Stephen's death he tempted to bring order to the situatic In 1046 he was killed by rebels w were trying to eradicate Christian from the country. He died somewh on the side of the Gellért Hill, wh rises to the south of Castle Hill. Lege has it that he was nailed into a barrel a rolled down into the Danube.

The rocky, limestone hill next to the L erty Bridge (**22**) is a protected area, has borne Gellért's name for centur There is an interesting chapel set cave in the hillside.

19

At the beginning of the 20th century Budapest was renowned for its graceful bridges (**19**), among other things, but no less for its thermal waters, which, gushing from springs or bore-holes, had been curing various ailments for thousands of years.

Before and during the First World War the *Gellért Baths,* which are incorporated in the Gellért Hotel, were built.
A miracle of Secessionist architecture, the Gellért Baths were successfully repaired following damage during the Second World War, and today await visitors in their former glory (**20-21**). Before 1990 many international meetings took place in the Gellért Hotel.

21

22

23

24

The old name of the sloping area between Castle Hill and th Gellért Hill was Rácváros ("Serb Quarter") or Tabán, i other words Tímártelep ("Tanners' Quarter"). The name c the northern part was Víziváros ("Water Town").
Both have very fine Baroque-style parish churches. The south ern one is dedicated to St Catherine of Alexandria, and th northern one to *St Anne* (**32**), but there are other churche of architectural interest, too (**25**). The Catholic churches a Baroque and the Reformed one Neo-Romanesque; the O thodox church was, alas, destroyed during the Second Wor War. The little houses of the Tabán have been knocked dow and street-vendors speaking regional German no long tempt passers-by with glasses of Danube water. Not that was ever advisable to drink it, anyway!

The baths of Tabán and Víziváros are famous. In addition the aristocratic Gellért Baths, several baths dating from Middle Ages and partly of Turkish construction (**26**) uti the hot, healing water of the springs. The Rudas, Rác, *Kir* and (a few minutes north of Víziváros) the Lukács baths places well worth visiting on account of their waters and torical atmosphere.
These two parts of the town are not over-rich in histo monuments, but there is a Rococo house where, allege Casanova once spent the night. Today visitors can still sp enjoyable nights in this area – for example, in the Cas which operates in an ornamented, church-like, former chine-house (**24**) of the former Royal Palace. This unu building and the *fable-like castle garden* above it were signed by Miklós Ybl, who also designed the Budapest O House. Formerly, carpet-sellers plied their wares in the s of the Castle Garden Bazaar; today statues are on dis there.

Northwest of Víziváros rises the Rózsadomb (Hill of Roses). Today this area is a byword for wealth, although villa construction here began only a century ago, encouraged by the whole some air and fine views. Earlier it was a countrified part, with viticulture and a clay quarry. Then it became a place of recreation, because pests destroyed a good part of Hungary's vines.

This part took its name from roses since a tomb there of a Turkish dervish who had lived a holy life became a place of pilgrimage for Muslims: this was Gül Baba, the "Father of Roses".

Picturesque *Gül Baba utca* (**27**), which leads up the side of the hill above the Lukács Baths, well indicates what the Rózsadomb was like before larger and smaller villas belonging to the old and new rich, and to diplomatic missions, populated its big and shady gardens. After 1990 a group of financiers seriously toyed with the idea of creating a Buda version of Grinzing somewhere here, on the Viennese model. However, entertainment districts only entertain when they develop organically, by themselves.

26

27

28

The Roman emperor Hadrian - who was responsible fo Hadrian's Wall in England and for the Castle of St Angel in Rome, and who suppressed the Bar-Kochba uprising in Ju daea - was as a young man governor of the province c Lower Pannonia (Pannonia Inferior Provincia) in the town c Aquincum. Perhaps it was he who built the Roman governor' palace whose ruins are to be found on Shipyard Island, venue for rock concerts in August.

Pannonia was an important part of the empire, a bord region occupied by powerful legions for four centuries. O the other side of the Danube the world of the Barbaricu began. On the edge of Europe stood a military camp and civilian town. The latter had two amphitheatres, baths, vill embellished with mosaics and frescoes (**29**), shops an workshops - as well as commercial links and equal status wi the town of Colonia, the modern Cologne. Tombstones – i cluding, after 325, an increasing number of Christian ones reflect the romanization of the province's Celtic inhabitant The remains of *Aquincum* are today on show as a separa *museum* (**28**). After 400 years of rule, Roman culture w forced to surrender this outpost of the empire: in 433 t Romans abandoned Pannonia to the Huns.

The *Margaret Island* also belonged to the province of Pa nonia. During the Middle Ages its Roman masonry was us in royal building operations. In was in the convent here t St Margaret, the daughter of Béla IV (1235–70), spent h brief life. Today the island (**30**) is a square kilometre of sha trees, grass, sports facilities, swimming-pools, hotels a paths – a huge leisure park for Budapest's children, famil and lovers.

29

31

32

After 1972 the United Nations' sci
tific and cultural administration exte
ed its famous World Heritage list.
In 1987 the Buda Castle District and
Pest and Buda Danube embankme
(**31**) were included in it.
But the *Parliament* (**32**), for example
not just an important political are
but one of Europe's finest Historic
style monuments.
At the same time the Classicist-s
Chain Bridge with Buda Castle Hill in
background is one of the best-knc
symbols of the Hungarian capital.
On the square in front of the Par
ment stand two statues depicting her
of liberty: Ferenc Rákóczi II (on ho
back), who fought against Habsburg
in 1703; and Lajos Kossuth (standi
who fought against it in 1849.

31

ıated above the Danube, the *Parlia-*
nt (**33**) offers a most impressive
w, despite the fact that from here
building's details cannot be seen
npletely. Around the outside of the
fice are eighty-eight statues of mon-
ıs – including the chieftains who led
Conquest, the early ruling princes
ıo did not yet possess Christian
wns), and the Hungarian princes of
ısylvania (a region given to Romania
920 and confirmed as Romanian in
7), who, between 1541 and 1699,
e rulers of a virtually independent
ıntry. Many of these statues are on
Danube side of the building. But the
ter was not too bothered with those
came to look: Imre Steindl had the
ues carved to immortalize the crafts-
of the Middle Ages.

33

34

Inside and outside, the embellishment on the *Hungarian Parliament*, which wa built between 1885 and 1904, serve a a real encyclopaedia of historic Hur gary. On the outside can be seen th coats of arms of the counties, as well a statues of former rulers; inside are rep resentations of crafts old and new (34

"In the interior decoration I drew on th flora of Hungary, the plant life of o fields, forests and plains," said Im Steindl, the building's designer. Beside important scenes from history, there a paintings showing hunting and fishin The monumentalism of the main stai case (**35**) well expresses the displ expected from the principal legislati assembly in Hungary, a country whi was then 1000 years old, 300,0C square kilometres in extent, and in t throes of dynamic development.
But this happy period lasted only o decade: when Franz Ferdinand, the h to the throne was struck down by assassin's bullet in Sarajevo, the Fi World War broke out.

35

'he two decades leading up to the First World War were the eyday of the Secession in Budapest. The principal master of ıis style was Ödön Lechner; everyone else either learnt from im or disowned him. One such was the *glass artist* and ıosaic designer *Miksa Róth* (**37**), who tried a create a lational Secession which went back to the supposed Orienıl roots of Hungarian art – to some kind of Persian-Hunnish 'adition. At this time, the theory – propounded in the ledieval chronicles – that the Hungarians were descendants f the Huns still enjoyed credence.

owever, it was not theory that lent charm to Lechner's works, r example the Hold utca *Post Office Savings Bank* (**36**) relling houses by Gaudí but designed independently of him, ıt rather the unmistakeable individuality of the master.

ıder Joseph II Pest began to spread northwards. When ɔpold II became king of Hungary in 1790, the new quar- received the name Lipótváros ("Leopold Town"). It was 'e that the building of the *Hungarian Academy of Sciences* 3) was erected, on the basis of plans by Friedrich August ller. (The Academy had been founded by Count István ·chenyi, a supporter of all kinds of economic and techni- modernization, and his friends in 1825.) Naturally, howr big the fine Neo-Renaissance building was, it served inly prestige purposes, and provided a home for the imtant Oriental Library. The Academy's research institutes 'e long since been unable to find sufficient space in the lding. On the square in front of the Academy stand :utes of two famous Hungarians: Count István Széchenyi, Academy's founder; and Ferenc Deák, who negotiated the mpromise between the Hungarian nation and the House of ɔsburg.

37

38

39

The earlier little church serving the paris
of Lipótváros suffered damage in 184
and, as a matter of fact, had become to
small for the district. Work on a ne
church began on a site formerly used fo
animal-fights, and construction was fir
in the Classical and then the Neo-R
naissance style (**39**). The *Basilica*, whic
was eventually finished in 1905, h
cathedral status.
The interior of the church (**40**) – whic
was named after St Stephen, Hungary
first king – was embellished in the secor
half of the 19th century with mosai
and murals by the best-known Hungar
an painters, and with sculptures by t
finest sculptors.

40

In the Basilica's Chapel of St Leopolc
kept the Hungarian nation's most j
ously guarded religious relic: the *H*
Dexter (**41**), the embalmed right hanc
St Stephen, the founder of the state.
day it is borne in procession around
neighbourhood on August 20, the
niversary of King Stephen's cano
ation in 1083. The story of the ro
right hand, taken and embalmed du
an early reburial of the king's body, is
adventurous one, as with most relics

It reached Buda in 1711, and was af
wards taken to Székesfehérvár, to a w
house used by Turkish merchants,
then to Dalmatia. Since 1971 its ho
has been the Chapel of St Leopold. (
reliquary – the container in which the
ic is kept – is 19th-century work.)

ı the 18th century Pest was Catholic ınd loyal to the Habsburgs, and was ıore of a German town than a Hungaan one. In addition to the Roman Catholics, only the Serbs and Greeks ould build places of worship within the own walls. For the Calvinists (who were ungarian speaking) this was not alwed, and for the Jews still less. An exeption was made for the mostly German-speaking Lutherans: they were able purchase a plot for a simple church **43**). Pest's Catholic character reained, and even in 1906 the Virgin Mary, in her capacity as Patroness of ungary, featured on the facade of the *urkish Bank building* (**42**) on Szervita r. Nevertheless in the Miksa Róth moic at the top of the modern building, e enthroned female figure already epicted the new god of bourgeois ogress, finance capital. This was the me capital that, in 1896, built Pest´s derground railway, the first on the ntinent of Europe.

42

43

44

45

With its allegorical figures (War, Pea Knowledge, Work, Welfare, Glory), t Archangel Gabriel holding the Cro of Lorraine and the Hungarian H Crown, the seven Hungarian chiefta on horseback, and behind them in semi-circle fourteen Hungarian kin ruling princes and statesmen, the *M lennial Monument* is a symbol of Bu pest. *Hősök tere* ("Heroes' Square where it stands, is the end point of e gant Andrássy út (**44**), built in the 19th century. A little further on ther a group of buildings bringing toget copies of monuments from Hungar past, with a leafy park all around.

To the right and left of the Millen Monument are museums. One, the *of Exhibitions* (**45**), presents cont porary art works to visitors in exh tions that are constantly changing, w the other, the Museum of Fine A displays works ranging from mas pieces of Antiquity to classics of 2C century European art.

/hen the Budapest *Opera House* was uilt (in the period1875–84) to plans y Miklós Ybl, it was obliged to comete with the Vienna Opera House, hich had opened in 1869.
iood railway links meant that Budapest pera fans could be in Viennal in four) five hours if they wished to see a ew production or to hear a famous nger. In Budapest, too, they wanted e best: Wagner and Verdi, Gounod, id the Hungarians Ferenc Erkel and íroly Goldmark.

47

48

t it was not just art that people nted; they wanted elegance, gilding, vet, and extravagant refreshments,) – in fact, a real palace on Sugár út, ich was later named Andrássy út, er Count Gyula Andrássy, Hungary's me minister following the Comprose. The new Opera House (**47**) was t one of the ornamented buildings 5) to be found along the avenue.
ch its easy grandeur, Miklós Ybl's in staircase in the Opera House (**48**) alls Charles Garnier's Paris Opera use of ten years earlier. The stage chinery was among the most modern ilable.

statues of Ferenc Liszt and Ferenc el were fashioned by Alajos Stróbl, oung master who had been trained /ienna. The murals, executed in the nantic style, are the work of Károly z, Bertalan Székely and Mór Than most famous Hungarian painters of age), and proclaim Budapest's dyiic development 100 years ago.

49

50

If a visitor to the city today wants experience what "the happy times peace" were like a century ago, he she should attend a concert at the *Ac emy of Music.* This college, which founded by Ferenc Liszt, is just a minutes' walk from the Opera. Great Hall, which has a fine-sou ing organ, offers excellent acous for concert-lovers, and those who Secessionist art can admire the Ala Körösfői-Kriesch mural (**49**) and Miksa Róth mosaics in the foyer. architecture is "frozen music".

After a concert, it is worth strol along Erzsébet körút to the New Y Coffee-house (**50**). Today, this is alm exactly as it was in 1894 when it op ed. At that time it was considered world's biggest coffee-house.
The higly-imaginative building was headquarters of an insurance comp which has long since disappeared.
The New York Coffee-house is a sh of modern Hungarian literature.

51

:er complained in 1941 that there would still be Jews in lapest when all the others in Europe had been banished to dagascar or to Siberia. As a matter of fact, right up until Second World War Jewish intellectuals and merchants upied an important place in Budapest's middle class.
synagogue, which combines Oriental and Byzantine ele- its, was built in 1859, in the so-called *Moorish style* – in locality where Theodor Herzl, who dreamt of a Jewish e, was born. The building, beautifully restored recently, designed by the Vienna architect Ludwig Förster.

However, the interior (**51**) was the work of Frigyes Feszl, the architect of the Romantic-style Vigadó. The synagogue, which is for Orthodox believers, was built by the renowned Viennese master Otto Wagner. Europe's largest synagogue, it was regarded as blasphemous by stricter Jews, since the pedals of its organ required pressing on the Sabbath and this constituted work.
At this time the synagogue's organ symbolized progress, as well as peaceful co-existence with the Christian community. There is a Jewish Museum in the synagogue building.

'he *Museum of Applied Arts* (**52**), ›pened in 1896 for the Millennial Celbrations, is just one Metro stop from he *Hungarian National Museum* (**54**), ne construction of which had been ompleted exactly fifty years before.

he Museum of Applied Arts, by Ödön echner, is in the Hungarian style (in ther words, it employs Indian and Peran decorative motifs), but is to some xtent inspired by English buildings in ne Romantic style. (There is a similar difice in Barcelona.)

he Hungarian National Museum was uilt by Mihály Pollack between 1837 nd 1846 for a collection established in 802. Like the British Museum, it could nly have been built in the Classical yle, since this symbolized the dignity an empire and of a nation awakening self-consciousness.

ırough the Hungarian National Musen the Kingdom of Hungary, independnt up until 1541, sought its place thin the Habsburg empire (after the eak of 1848, for a few months outle the empire, too). But in 1867 the ›mpromise occurred, and almost five cades of development and relative nquillity followed. Then, with the outeak of the First World War, the "long" 'th century ended and a new world era gan.

ose who want better to understand ngary's somewhat complex history in its livelinesss are best advised to visthe new historical exhibition at the ngarian National Museum.

gether with the Budapest History ıseum (in the Castle District) which sents the history of the capital, this ıtes the events of the past thousand rs in the Carpathian Basin – in other rds, the story of "old" Hungary.

eorganized and augmented archaeoical exhibition presenting an exnely rich selection of material is curtly under preparation.

Holy Crown of Hungary (**53**) symzes the country itself. Except at onation ceremonies, before the Sec World War its gold bands embeled with enamel and pearls were seen on special occasions, and then just elected dignitaries.

Coronation Insignia are housed in a ırate room.

53

54

55

Formerly, Pest was the area within th
old town wall. The first Christian churc
there may have been built from th
masonry of the old Roman fortication
Next to the Elizabeth Bridge, rebui
after the Second World War, is th
Church of the Inner Town (**55**), th
third church on the site but still th
oldest in Pest. It was here that St Gellér
the spiritual advisor to King Stephen
son Prince Imre, was buried after h
martyrdom in 1046. (A statue of St Ge
lért on the Gellért Hill across the riv
looks onto the church.)
Today's Gothic edifice was built mo
than 600 years ago by Sigismund
Luxembourg's master-masons.
Inside a few very fine marble reliefs r
call the splendour of the Renaissanc
and a *mihrab*, a Muslim prayer-nich
reminds visitors that in the 17th cent
ry the church was used as a mosque.
The west front, today's altars and t
quire were built in the Baroque a
Classical styles after 1725.
In the first half of the 19th century t
church was surrounded by little sho
Only in the 20th century was the bui
ing's architectural significance realiz
and full-scale restoration took place
late as 1970.

56

"The World of Yesterday", as Stefan Zweig in his memoirs called this period, receded into the past during the First World War. Today Neoconservative thinkers are trying to resurrect its best traditions from the watery grave of the revolutions. This short pedestrian precinct is living European history – a relic of an entire earlier world, and not just of old Pest.

One of Pest's most interesting old buildings is *Párizsi-udvar,* 'Paris Arcade' (**58**), on Ferenciek tere, named after the Franciscan church there. A former savings bank, it is today a fairy-tale castle of offices, studios and apartments with exciting ground-plans.
This building is an example of the Oriental-type covered shopping arcade fashionable in European capitals around the turn of the 20th century. Its designer was an architect of imaginative genius, the Hamburg-born Henrik Schmahl, a foreman who rose to become the head of construction work on the Opera House, and who subsequently dreamt up Eastern fairy-tale palaces for the city of Pest.

59

ıciek tere and *Kígyó utca* (**56**) cut *Váci utca* (**59**), an ınt Inner Town shopping street, into two parts.
ígyó utca the prosperity of the rich years from the turn ıe 20th century up until the outbreak of the First World is reflected in the embellishment of the buildings (**57**).

the shops beckon: carpets, antiques, various French ımes, porcelain, expensive pipes and tobacco products, fine textiles are on show in every shop window – while urniture and fittings of the pharmacies are of a kind nor- found only in museums.

60

Lajos Márk, a painter once fashionab and popular in America, executed a S cessionist-style mural in the *Philanth* ("shop for lovers of flowers" - **60**), o of Váci utca's most atmospheric c shops.

On the buildings between Vörösmar tér and Kígyó utca the visitor can s examples of every 19th- and 20th-ce tury architectural style, from Classici through the Secession and Art Deco the emergence of the Bauhaus. In fa *Váci utca* (**61**) is something of an chitectural guide-book, although it c only really be used as such in the ve early morning. Nevertheless, from mo ing to evening the streetscape is det mined by strollers, onlookers and sho pers, and (as in every metropolis) some ladies and gentlemen of not peccable morals.

Fashion in Pest has always been dicta by the shops located in Váci utca a in the streets which lead off from it. Váci utca has always been Budapes Bond Street, regardless of the curr political climate.

61

62

63

-cially Vörösmarty tér is situated
side the real Inner Town and is al-
-ly Lipótváros, since it lies to the
-th of the earlier town gate.

-ually, it constitutes the heart of the
-r Town, especially with regard to the
-beaud Pattiserie (**62**). In today's
-na only traces remain of the ambi-
- associated with the old Austro-
-garian Monarchy – the ambience
-lled by Gerbeaud's. A coffee-house
pattiserie have operated here since
1. The Swiss-born Gerbeaud, who
a Knight of France's Legion of
-our, invented cherry bonbons.
-950, for legal reasons, Gerbeaud's
-renamed the Vörösmarty, after that
- dramatic of Hungarian poets Mi-
Vörösmarty, whose white-marble
-e can be seen on the square.

- a cup of coffee and a cake in the
-e-house, Pest citizens would stroll
- the *Danube Corso* (**63**), or, from
-nfortable seat, admire the Buda sky-
which as early as 1480 enthralled
-llustrator of the most important
-raphical guidebook of that time.
-hey could also look at the Vigadó.

The *Vigadó*, designed in an Oriental a Romantic style by Frigyes Feszl and e bellished with *statues* (**64**) by Kár Alexy, was so badly damaged during Second World War that its full resto tion was completed only in 1980 – w two auditoriums, a gallery and a ple ant restaurant. Today foreign visitors the Vigadó area will encounter m vendors, waiters, guides and especi other foreign visitors than they will g uine Budapest citizens, but this is pr ably unavoidable.

In front of the row of hotels, built on sites of older hotels destroyed in Second World War, there is a sculpt displaying the somewhat ironical wi Pest's inhabitants: the *Little Princ* (**65**). László Márton's alarmingly sized and lifelike bronze figure sits the railings. The little girl seems to laughing at the hustle and bustle of world. History has taught her that s ous things have their amusing side. example, a little further along stands Classicist-style Chain Bridge. In 184 was finished but not opened, yet there were some who wanted to blo up. In 1945 others actually did blo up. In streets far from the river there plaques which show the height reac by the icy floodwaters when the Dan burst its banks in 1838, swee proud Pest away, including house wealthy merchants and powerful l owners.

Budapest is a somewhat older Vienna, and during the Second W War it suffered almost as much as saw. The scars inflicted by tank car in 1956 were soon removed, but pock-marks caused by the machine fire remained. Budapest was capture Tatars and Turks. Subsequently, it occupied by the multinational troo the Holy Roman Empire (Christian mittedly, but not renowned for thei bearance), and later still by Austr Germans and Russians. Even pric 1944 it had experienced a dozen r or minor sieges, and those taking p various uprisings were always hap congregate here.
Budapest is not simply a beautiful but beautiful *despite all these th* Perhaps this explains why it is so loved.